7 Things You Must Do

to be an Effective Small Group Leader

www.tonywolfe.net

Scripture quotations are taken from the Christian Standard Bible.

Table of Contents

INTRODUCTION

Since 1999 it has been my joy to serve in various forms of small group leadership in local Southern Baptist churches. Since 2017, that joy has multiplied as I travel around the state of Texas coaching, training, and consulting with churches of every size and ethnicity. I believe that healthy small groups make healthy churches.

Some of the most exciting times in my ministry came as a small group leader. However, some of the most challenging times in my ministry also came as a small group leader. There is something so *real* about investing yourself in a small group of people over the course of many years. Corporate worship services are powerful—the time spent singing together, praying together, and listening to the Word of God preached together. Awesome. But doing life together in small groups is where you learn who people really are. You learn what makes them tick. You learn what sets them off. You learn what they are passionate about. You learn areas in which they deeply struggle. You learn the good qualities of their personalities. You learn the annoying qualities of their personalities. Church life together gets *real* in small groups.

Your church may organize small groups in a number of different ways and call them by a number of different titles. You may have "cell groups," "discipleship groups," "home groups," "Sunday School," "life groups," or "community groups." They may meet on Sunday mornings, Sunday nights, Wednesday nights, or another night of the week. They may be held in homes, at the church facilities, at a local business, or in a park somewhere. Whatever you call them, and whenever and wherever they meet, small groups are vital to the effectiveness of your church. And as the leader of a small group, you have been afforded the privilege and responsibility of investing in people over time so that they might grow up in Christlikeness. Discipleship, evangelism, ministry, worship, fellowship—for those under your spiritual care, you facilitate all of the church's purposes on a more personal level than your pastoral staff will ever be able to. Small groups are the backbone of the local church. Your role as leader is essential to the success of your church's mission. Thank God for you!

This book will focus only on practical responsibilities of the leader's role in church-based small groups. Instead of taking the space to establish certain essential truths, allow me to begin by stating five foundational assumptions that guide the practical responsibilities of the small group leader. These are "I will..." statements of core commitment that form the foundation for small group leadership in the local church.

ONE: I will uphold that the Bible is the authoritative, inspired, inerrant, infallible Word of God. The practices suggested in this guide will make little sense to you if you do not agree that the Bible is what it claims to be. In discipleship, we teach people the Bible. If your people are to grow up in Christ and align their hearts more closely with the Father's heart, the Bible will be the curriculum, the Holy Spirit the Teacher, and you the mouthpiece (megaphone at times) and the model of biblical truth.

TWO: I will serve humbly, devotedly, and seriously. All leadership in the local church is *servant* leadership. This was Jesus's model, so it is our standard. If you have become a leader because you would rather lead than follow, hang it up today. If you cannot follow, you cannot lead. If you cannot learn, you cannot teach. The best small group leaders are those who are humble before God and before those under their care, devoted to weekly tasks required, and serious about the long-term spiritual growth of their people.

THREE: I will regularly participate in church activities. Not out of obligation but rather, from a heart of sincere devotion. Your small group is not God's gift to your church. It is one piece of a very big puzzle. It is a vital piece, no doubt, but still only one piece. When small groups become Christian clubs, church members become perpetual consumers. But God's design is that church members actually produce something within the Body. You need to get your people mobilized for the mission, not comfortable in their cushions. And what you model will be what they will do. In other words, if you don't they won't. There is no better way to ignite within your people a devotion to your church than by actively participating in church activities and encouraging your people to do the same.

FOUR: I will treat this role as a shepherding responsibility in the Body of Christ. Your senior pastor is the lead under-shepherd of the church, but you are an under-shepherd of him— an extension of his ministry. You are to provide soul care for the sheep God has given you. Small group leadership is not an outlet to show people how much of the Bible you know and how super-spiritual you are. It is a petri dish for spiritual growth—a place where leaders get on their hands and knees to wash the feet of their disciples. In many ways, small groups provide the best structure in a church for person-to-person ministry. This is about so much more than teaching a weekly lesson. If you are not committed to loving people and shepherding them with grace and endurance, you have signed up for the wrong role in the church body.

FIVE: I will support the vision of the church leadership and the direction of the church body. This is not about building your kingdom. It's about building God's kingdom.

Small group leaders serve under the umbrella of the church's leadership. Small group leaders who cannot support the vision and direction of the church leadership will always find themselves creating conflict and stirring up division within the church body. Instead of vertebrae in a healthy backbone structure, these groups ultimately become amputated appendages over whom the rest of the Body regularly trips and stumbles. If you cannot support the leadership of your church body, it is best for you to step aside and allow someone else to lead your small group.

If you can agree to these five "I will..." statements then you are ready to proceed to the following chapters. Keep in mind that these are practical responsibilities that you *must do* in order to be an effective small group leader.

Chapter 1
Pray for Your People

"We always thank God for you, making mention of you constantly in our prayers."
1 Thessalonians 1:2

I knew conflict was brewing. Most Sunday mornings you could cut the tension in our room with a butter knife. Two of the couples in my small group had a minor disagreement between them that seemed to be escalating rather quickly. I saw the way they avoided eye contact. I noticed one of the couples slacking from regular attendance. Then I started hearing the whispers in little circles; sides had been formed, loyalties staked, and somehow the truth had gotten lost in all of the polarized secrecy. I had no clue what to do. I was sure that my small group was closing in on complete implosion. So

I began to pray. I prayed for the two couples every day, and sometimes multiple times a day. I prayed for God to unveil the truth, cut through the lies, break hearts for restoration, and heal the division in our group.

The call to leadership on any level in the church is a call to consistent, heartfelt, devotional prayer. James writes that the prayer of a righteous person is very powerful in its effect (James 5:16). Those in leadership positions are to be carefully considered by the church staff, to ensure that they are living out the righteousness God has imputed to them in Christ Jesus. Perfection will not be an accurate description of such a person, but increasing righteousness should be evident. Those who are living out the righteousness of Christ in a leadership position are responsible for prayers of faith. They are entrusted with the great responsibility of regularly interceding for those under their care, listening to the Holy Spirit's insight and pleading for God's sanctifying graces in every circumstance.

After about two weeks of devoted, focused prayer toward this end I noticed a change in the atmosphere of our group setting. The polarized division seemed to be dissipating. Two more weeks passed before I found out that the two couples had met together on their own, worked through the issues, and agreed to set aside their differences so as not to hinder God's work in and through our small group. Imagine that. Prayer works.

In the middle of my rejoicing over that victory, a simple prompting from God's Spirit hit me like a Mack truck on an open highway. Why had I not been praying for these couples all along? Why did I wait for the lid to blow before I considered their personal lives worthy of my time in devoted prayer? How much of this problem could have been avoided if I was proactive in prayer for my people instead of reactive? How many similar opportunities had I missed? What other lives had I failed by not regularly praying for them when they were under my spiritual care? I learned a valuable lesson from that occasion. Daily, focused prayer for the people under my care is necessary for effective leadership. There is no shortcut to this. No substitution for it. No way to delegate it. No excuse for relegating it. No Spirit-filled leadership without it.

This is a call to reconsider the nature of your prayer life, as a leader within the Body of Christ. Most often, our prayer lives are merely reactive. Something goes wrong, and we pray for God to fix it. Unintentionally, God becomes to us little more than the church plumber or air conditioner repair man. Fix-it God. God in a box. We leaders consider ourselves the spiritual ones when we take people's problems and crises to the Lord in prayer. But as a small group leader, if your prayer is merely reactive, you need to refocus your prayer life immediately.

Change from reactive prayer to proactive prayer. Go ahead and assume that Satan is prowling around like a roaring lion, seeking whom he might devour. Go ahead and assume that he and the demons of Hell are actively engaged in the marriages, family lives, jobs, hobbies, and social circles of the people under your care. And pray with devotion for the power of Almighty God to protect them from the evil one. Jesus prayed this for his small group before the hour of testing came (John 17:15). Seeing the enemy's hand at work in the life of Peter, our Lord also prayed specifically for this disciple, that his faith would not fail and that the lessons he learned in repentance would later serve to strengthen the group as a whole (Luke 22:31-32).

As the leader of your small group, you must regularly pray for the people under your care. Here are three areas of prayer focus that you need to make a daily part of your ministry to every person in your small group:

1. Pray for their spiritual health. The overarching goal for a small group is to facilitate guided transformation into Christlikeness through long-term investment in people's lives. If you have 5-20 people in your small group, then you have 5-20 people who—every day—are battling forces of Hell, wrestling with areas of obedience to God's Word, and evaluating the claims of godless philosophies which barrage them from every angle all day long. Pray that God will give your people victory over the evil one, endurance in submitting to biblical truth, and a Christ-centered worldview to see clearly through the smoke of unbiblical thoughts and ideas on every front.

As their small group leader, you will often be the first to know of specific areas of spiritual struggle in their lives. You will be on the front line of offense and/or defense when one of your people is wrestling with faithfulness in evangelism, servant-heartedness in ministry, strongholds of addiction, or questions of purpose. Pray for them. Faithfully. Every one of them.

2. Pray for their families. Learn their spouses' and children's names, and listen when they tell you the things their family members are struggling through. One of the most encouraging things you can say to someone throughout the week is that you've been praying for their family members by name— that is, if you actually have been praying for their family members by name. Servant leadership means that when your heart hurts, my heart hurts. And where is a source of more frequent pain that within the walls of one's own home?

Paul wrote in 1 Corinthians 12:26, "So if one member suffers, all the members suffer with it; if one member is honored, all the members rejoice with it." Pray for their family like it was your own family. Of all the things that impact your people's commitment to the church body and forward spiritual progress, the family is at the top of the list. If Satan cannot pry his way into your small group, he will pry his way into the families of your small group members. Pray for the families of your people. Pray for them by name. And pray for them like it matters.

3. Pray for their other relationships. Although I may have never met you personally and have no clue that you are reading this book right now, I am going to make an educated guess: your church is not the perfect church. Shocking how I knew, right? Paul instructs us in Ephesians 4:2-3 to "walk worthy" of our calling, "with all humility and gentleness, with patience, accepting one another in love, diligently keeping the unity of the Spirit with the peace that binds us." The apostle admits that when you sign up for community in a body of believers, you can expect opportunities to be gentle and patient with others. Why? Because like you, they are not perfect people.

In a small group, people will regularly be offended by others. They will be wronged. Their patience will be tested. And so will yours. The solution? Diligence, says Paul. Be a diligent peace keeper. And how are you, a human agent, to protect such a lofty ideal between two other people? Paul did it through prayer. Just before Ephesians 4:2-3, Paul discloses that he prays constantly for those under his spiritual care – that they would "know the Messiah's love," as a prerequisite for being "filled with all the fullness of God," (see Eph. 3:14-19).

As a small group leader you need to regularly pray for your people. Not only that the Holy Spirit would be the uncontested occupant of the space of each of their hearts—but that He would also occupy the space between their hearts and the hearts of others. All people are real people with real problems. Because of this, every single day your people struggle with relationships in their circle of influence. You need to be a prayer warrior for those relationships. Pray that their conversations, interactions, and offenses would be covered by the grace of God.

PRACTICAL TIPS:

• At the beginning of the week, make notecards for each of your small group members. Write the person or couples' name on the top of the card. On the left side of the card, list these four areas for prayer focus, skipping a space between each: (1) Spiritual Health, (2) Family, (3) Relationships, and (4) Other. At the beginning of the week, write yourself short notes for each area of prayer focus. Use these cards to guide your daily prayers for your people over the next week. Consider praying over each card every day, or at least for two-three cards daily.

• If you do not know any specifics about one of your group members' needs, call, message, or text to ask how you can pray for him or her this week.

• Be consistent. Get up 10 minutes earlier, stay up 10 minutes later, or carve out 10 minutes of your lunch break every day, and stick to it. Consistency in my prayer life is never better than when I find a specific daily time that works for me, and protect it vigorously.

• When someone in your group catches you in the hallway or after the group meeting to ask you to pray for something specific, do two things immediately: (1) Ask, "Can we pray for that together right now?" and bow together in a short prayer for that concern. (2) When you get a couple of seconds, jot down the prayer concern somewhere—anywhere—then transfer it to your notecard when you get a chance.

• If prayer is needed for a specific event, surgery, opportunity, or meeting, set a reminder on your phone to pray for that concern as it is happening. Consider sending a short text to let your group member know you are praying for him or her in the moment. If appropriate, follow up with the group member later that evening or the next day.

• In your daily Bible reading, if a Scripture verse pops out at you as relevant to a group member's prayer need, consider doing a few things: (1) jot down the reference on their notecard to remind you, (2) pray that Scripture over him or her daily, and/or (3) send a quick text or message to the group member including encouragement from that Scripture.

Your time is valuable, I know. It takes discipline and devotion to develop an effective prayer life. But as a small group leader, this is something you *must do* to be effective. In the next chapter, we will evaluate the importance of being intentional about teaching the content (Bible/curriculum) during small group gatherings.

NOTES:

CHAPTER 2
Teach the Content

"All Scripture is inspired by God and is profitable for teaching, for rebuking, for correcting, for training in righteousness, so that the man of God may be complete, equipped for every good work."
2 Timothy 3:16-17

Over the years, my education and experience in low brass has afforded me many connections with local high school band directors. In one particular city as I got to know a local high school band director, I learned more and more of the things he despised about his job. He loved to teach kids that wanted to be in band, but he absolutely loathed teaching Music Appreciation classes. These were for students who were not in band or choir, but needed the course to satisfy the Arts requirement in their degree plan. Occasionally I would walk in on his Music Appreciation class and the kids would all be sitting scattered throughout the room with their phones out and ear-buds in. I asked him one day, "What are they doing?" to which he facetiously replied, "They are appreciating music."

I don't think that's exactly what the State of Texas's course designers had in mind when they were developing the curriculum for this Music Appreciation course. I also seriously doubt that the activities in this man's classroom could have been justified anywhere in the TEKS (Texas Essential Knowledge and Skills). They met for almost an hour every day. Music was there, in the room. Each of them appreciated what he or she *wanted* to appreciate about music. But ultimately, the curriculum was not being taught. These young people had given hours of their day to gather together throughout the year, but at the end of the year, they had learned nothing of value.

Sadly, this can also be true of a church's small group gatherings. When announcements, prayer requests, and friendly banter take up too much of the allotted gathering time, we have a problem. Similarly, an unprepared or uncommitted teacher can easily take group discussions where they do not need to go. My band teacher friend showed no commitment to the curriculum because he saw no value in it, himself. And instead of using the time gathered to make worthy investments in the lives of his people, he allowed other things to take center stage.

Consider with me the surpassing value of knowing and living God's Word, as understood by the author of Psalm 119:

> "How happy are those whose way is blameless, who walk according to the Lord's instruction! Happy are those who keep his decrees and seek him with all their heart," (vs.1-2).

> "If only my ways were committed to keeping your statutes!" (v.5).

> "How can a young man keep his way pure? By keeping your word... I have treasured your word in my heart so that I may not sin against you," (vs.9-11).

> "Open my eyes so that I may contemplate wondrous things from your instruction," (v.18).

> "My life is down in the dust; give me life through your word," (v.25).

"I am weary from grief; strengthen me through your word," (v.28).

"Turn my heart to your decrees," (v.36).

"Never take the word of truth from my mouth, for I hope in your judgments," (v.43).

"I rise at midnight to thank you for your righteous judgments," (v.62).

"It was good to be afflicted so that I could learn your statutes," (v.71).

"I long for your salvation; I put my hope in your words," (v.81).

"Give me life in accordance with your faithful love, and I will obey the decree you have spoken," (v.88).

And this, up to verse 88, only takes us halfway through the chapter. What your small group members need is a steady diet of God's Word. They need to know it, to own it, and to live it. Over the course of a few years you and your group should journey together through the whole Bible, feasting on the grand buffet of God's revelation. The riches of his faithful love are revealed in His written Word. When we do not take seriously the responsibility of learning and living it, we become spiritually anorexic, biblically emaciated, our souls wasting away from spiritual malnourishment.

Small group gatherings too often resemble my band director friend's Music Appreciation class: the Bible is present and people are appreciating what they *want* to appreciate about it—but the curriculum of God's Word is not being taught systematically. This works against the purpose of your group, not for it. Here are a few points of necessity in order for you to be effective in leading your small group to diligently study God's Word when you are gathered together.

1. Each week, encounter the material yourself in a meaningful, transformative way. Teach the lesson to yourself before you teach it to your learners. You have to allow the truths of God's Word to invade your life before you can expect God to use you in allowing His Word to invade the lives of your group members. My band director friend did not teach the curriculum content because he saw no value in it. Make sure that before you stand before your group to teach anything from the Word of God, you see the value in it. Read through the biblical text several times. Pray for God to open your spiritual eyes and ears so that you don't miss the deep things of God. Ask yourself questions about the text, and find answers. Pray that the Lord will give you opportunities to live it before you teach it.

2. Pray for the Holy Spirit to do the teaching in your group meetings. You might have the title and the responsibility, but the Holy Spirit is the only One who has the power to impress the truth of God's Word on the hearts of your group members. The Holy Spirit is the teacher, who guides the Christian into all truth (John 16:13). Consider Paul's words to the church in Corinth: "Now we have not received the spirit of the world, but the Spirit who comes from God, so that we may understand what has been freely given to us by God," (1 Cor. 2:12).

The Holy Spirit takes God's Word and gives the believer understanding. The Holy Spirit is the true Teacher in your classroom. Every week you need to bathe your lesson and your room in prayer, asking Him to do what only He can do, and giving Him room to do it.

3. Make the lesson about the Bible, not the printed study guide. The Holy Spirit is the Teacher; the Bible is the curriculum. Printed study guides are valuable tools for every small group. The right tools can help you navigate through the Bible in an organized, systematic way. Most churches provide some kind of material (tools) for small group teachers. The church's leaders are the ones who are ultimately responsible for the teaching of God's Word that takes place under the umbrella of their leadership. So use the tools provided. But understand that the tools are just tools.

Your group members need to be engaging the biblical text itself week after week, month after month, and year after year. The illustrations, discussion questions, and guided thoughts of your study guide's writers are very helpful in applying the truth of God's Word in a timely and relevant way. But as the group leader, be careful to place more emphasis on what God's Word says than on what the study guide author says.

4. Be prepared. When you have not prepared for the lesson, your group can tell. When they perceive this, it communicates to them that this content and this gathering was not worth your time in preparation. If it was not worth your time in preparation, it is not worth their time in application.

Your calling as a small group leader is a huge responsibility. Just think of the gravity of it all. Your have been entrusted with the systematic biblical discipleship of a group of people. God wants to use you as His mouthpiece—His vehicle—of biblical truth week after week, pouring into the hearts and minds of His children. The biblical writer James takes this very seriously: "Not many of you should become teachers, my brothers, knowing that we will receive a stricter judgment, for we all stumble in many ways. If anyone does not stumble in what he says, he is a mature man who is able to control his whole body," (Ja. 3:1-2).

Your group members will take what you say in your meeting every week and directly associate it with God's eternal truth. Paul instructs Timothy, "Be diligent to present yourself approved to God, a worker who doesn't need to be ashamed, correctly teaching the word of truth," (2 Ti. 2:15).

When you stand before your group every week, you are standing before God as well. Be sure to present yourself to Him approved, cutting His Word straight and representing Him accurately. This takes diligence in preparation.

The weekly gathering times of your small

group must have at their center the diligent, systematic teaching of God's Word. With so many other things going on in your life and in the lives of your people, this is often more difficult than it sounds. Below are some practical tips to help you diligently teach the content of God's Word week after week.

PRACTICAL TIPS:

• Develop for yourself a system of study/preparation that works for you. Perhaps you read the entire lesson and biblical text on Monday, work through the discussion questions on Tuesday, then study the parts of the lesson individually Wednesday through Friday. Maybe your time for study is immediately after your personal devotional time every day, or maybe it is at a different time of day. Maybe you have a couple of hours Thursdays or Fridays during which you can completely devote yourself to preparing for the lesson, instead of working on it every day. Find a system that works for you, and stick with it.

• As you walk your group through the lesson, consider sharing with them how it impacted you personally as you studied. Two rules of thumb here: (1) Make your personal testimonies and illustrations short, and only do this occasionally. Too much of this makes the lesson about you instead of the biblical text. (2) Try not to use yourself as a positive example. This can give off an appearance of pride or superiority, even if that is not your intention.

• Stick to the lesson plan. Especially if you have a group that is prone to discussion, you may have to gently redirect conversation back to the lesson at times. Remember, the point of the gathering is not just to get people talking. The point is to get them thinking and conversing *about the biblical text at hand*. The small group gathering is not a place for personal vendettas, soap-boxes, or opinion-stroking; neither from the leader, nor from the group members.

When necessary, use gentle conversational redirectors such as, "The question was '_____;' do you think we answered the question?" or "This is such a good discussion; let's put it on hold for now so that we can give God's Word the attention it deserves today, and we'll get back to that discussion another time."

• Before you start the lesson in group meetings, pray. Pray for communicated prayer concerns, yes. But make sure to devote time in your prayer every week to ask the Holy Spirit to guide the group into the truth of the text for the day. That audible prayer together will do two things: It will (1) invite God's manifest presence into the lesson and into the room to do what only He can do, and (2) set the tone for approaching God's Word with reverence and expectation.

The Word of God is the curriculum. Study guides, commentaries, and other publications are great tools that help draw out the truths of God's Word in a fresh and applicable way. But they are only tools—means to an end.

For the progressive sanctification of your people, what they need more than anything else is consistent, diligent, systematic encounters in God's Word. The Holy Spirit will do the teaching if you will let Him. But you must do your part in preparation and presentation.

NOTES:

Chapter 3
Don't Waste Time

*"Pay careful attention, then, to how you live—
not as unwise people but as wise—making the
most of the time, because the days are evil."*
Ephesians 5:15-16

The devoted Christian couple was new to the area and looked forward to Sunday morning when they would attend a church in their neighborhood for the first time. They had browsed the church website a few days earlier and found the times for small group Bible study and worship service. Sunday morning they got up early and dressed nicely, got the children in the car, and set out on their way. They arrived to church five minutes early to get their children situated in their own small group rooms. Then the church's Welcome Center volunteer led them down a separate hallway to a room where the small group their age would be meeting.

To their dismay, there was no one else in the room. They decided to go to the restroom and grab a cup of coffee, then come back. Five minutes later—five minutes after the group meeting was *supposed* to start—they walked back into the classroom to find only one other couple and the group leader.

Introductions were made. Small talk commenced. Three other couples made their way into the room over the next ten minutes. The group leader made several announcements then asked for prayer requests. The prayer was quick. Then he lobbed out an icebreaker question. By the time the group turned their attention to the actual biblical text, there were only twenty-five minutes left. The new couple felt like the group leader and regular attenders had wasted their time. Next week, they would try to find a different group, or maybe a different church altogether.

Time is valuable. In fact, in our culture it is our people's most prized possession. When people entrust the church with their time, it is imperative that church leaders honor that sacrifice by making the most of every minute. This is not to say that the meeting needs to be rushed or that it should follow a rigid minute-by-minute structure. It is a simple acknowledgement of the sacrifice your people are making every week when they give you their time. It is a matter of good stewardship from you as their servant leader.

Here are several basic guidelines for time management in weekly group meetings. You would be wise to follow these guidelines, if you are to be an effective small group leader.

1. Start on time. When you advertise a start time for your small group meeting, start at that time. I wish the example at the beginning of this chapter was a hypothetical one. However, it has been an all to common complaint from guests in small groups at the churches where I have served. As group members become more and more comfortable around one another, they tend to burn time at the beginning of the gathering by catching up on family and work-related conversations. The more the group leader allows this lag-time at the beginning of meetings, the longer that lag-time gets.

This is a constant struggle, and it requires your constant attention. But I promise, if you have guests (and the goal is that you will), they are looking at their watches and wondering why they showed up on time. And if you have group members who are showing up on time regularly, they will begin to show up later and later, or not at all. Start on time.

2. End on time. There is very rarely a good reason to keep your group longer than the time you have allotted. When you advertise an end time for your group meeting, your people expect the meeting to end on time. They have plans afterward. Their children are waiting in the hallways or in the classrooms of the children's wing. Their food is burning in the crockpot. Their teenager is sitting in the hot car waiting for them to come out. They need to get to the choir room to warm up for the service. They have responsibilities at the welcome center, at the media booth, or in the nursery.

If you constantly abuse the time that your people give you by keeping them too long, they will stop coming. This is just a simple matter of basic time management during your group meetings. Start on time and end on time. Your people's time is to be honored, never wasted and never taken advantage of.

3. Occasionally evaluate/audit your use of the time allotted in the weekly group

meeting. Have your spouse or a trusted friend in the group take note of the time you spent on various components. Or maybe just think back through the discussions and conversations during the lesson to evaluate whether or not the main points of the content were adequately addressed. Often, poor time management on one point in the lesson leads to a lack of sufficient time for another point in the lesson.

A friend asked me to do this for him once, as he taught our small group over the course of a month. At the end of the month, I showed him my notes and he was completely shocked. Not only had he begun speaking an average of 7 minutes late, he had also spent an average of 23 minutes on announcements and prayer requests at the beginning of group time. He was wondering why he never had enough time to get through the lessons. As it turns out he had prepared 50-minute lessons, but by the time he actually got to the text each week he only had 20 minutes to get through it.

4. Allot yourself time segments for different components of your weekly group gathering and lesson plan. For example: 5 minutes for prayer requests and prayer, 5 minutes to introduce the lesson, 15 minutes for point one, 15 minutes for point two, 15 minutes for point three and 5 minutes to wrap-up and close. You don't have to follow these rigidly. If good, on-topic discussion is happening in point one, allow it to go a little longer and shave some time off of point two or three. If you know a particular question in point three will generate discussion in your group, shave some time off of point one or two by cutting out an illustration or choosing to ask less discussion questions.

Many leaders' guides offer suggested time allotments for sections of every lesson. These may or may not work for you. But at least think through them and adjust them for your group if necessary.

PRACTICAL TIPS:

• If your group has developed a culture of starting late, you may need to address it head-on. Begin by apologizing for being a poor manager of their time in the past, and indicate your sincerest intentions to better honor their time in the future. Explain to your people that you are inviting and expecting guests every single week. Consider reading or paraphrasing this chapter's opening illustration to them. Don't make it embarrassing for anyone, and don't do this with a negative tone. Simply explain that beginning next week, you are going to do everything in your power to start on time. If they get there late, that's no problem—they can come right in.

• Wear a watch. I know, that's obvious. But you might be surprised how many small group leaders begin a lesson every week with no way of monitoring the time. If you're not a watch-wearing person, get a decent size clock to set up across the room from you (facing you), at eye-level. This allows you to keep the flow of the lesson going and maintain good eye contact with your people, while still monitoring the clock.

I have a friend who uses a count-down clock app on his phone when he preaches: green numbers counting from his target time frame down to 0, then red numbers in the negative counting the seconds and minutes he goes over.

• Minimize or cut out announcements. Do not read through the church's announcements during your small group's meeting time. Those announcements are most likely listed on the bulletin, scrolling on the screen before service, featured on the website, and shared among friends on social media. If a church leader asks you to announce something in your group, do it very quickly at the beginning or end of your time together. Usually there is no need for discussion concerning such announcements. Likewise, announcements specific to your group should be made quickly and concisely. If plans need to be made for upcoming group events, missions, ministries, or gatherings, do that at the end of class after the lesson. If time does not permit, make those plans in a Facebook closed group or a group text message or email.

• Don't bite off too much in one lesson. Usually, published lessons for small groups are designed in such a way that you can choose which illustrations and discussion questions you want to use in your group meeting. If you have a group that does not discuss things as openly/freely, then you may need to use more of the guide's options. Sometimes you may be able to come up with a different discussion question altogether that you know will resonate with your group members and keep them on-target conversationally.

If you have a group that likes to discuss things at length, be selective about which and how many discussion questions to ask. It is not important that you get to all of the guide's illustrations and questions. Consider these as options, not requirements. It is important, however, that you give the biblical text the time and attention it deserves—both in explanation and application.

To be an effective small group leader, you must be a wise manager of your time during group meetings. When group leaders waste their people's time, they minimize their effectiveness in teaching biblical content and they disrespect the sacrifices that their group members have made in coming to the meeting. Start the meeting on time. Manage the meeting time. End the meeting on time. Do this weekly, and you will honor the investments your people have made through their devoted regular attendance.

Time management is very important, but the leader must also learn how to engage the group effectively during that time frame. Chapter 4 will deal with this next essential component of effective small group leadership.

NOTES:

CHAPTER 4
Be Engaging

"Now may the God of hope fill you with
all joy and peace as you believe
so that you may overflow with hope by the
power of the Holy Spirit."
Romans 15:13

"You've got to be kidding me," I thought to myself as the pastor moved to point number three of his sermon that morning. He was there in view of a call; after the morning worship service, the church would vote on whether or not he was to be our next pastor. But during his sermon, he never once looked up from his notes. He read every single word straight off the page. I kept thinking, "Maybe he's just nervous. Maybe it will get better." But as he moved into his third point still reading word for word from his notes, I lost that hope. It was all I could do to stay awake. "He should just print this out and hand us all a copy," I thought to myself. "I can read. This has got to be the most boring sermon I have ever heard in my life."

When it comes to teaching a small group lesson, it's not just reading off the page that makes teaching boring (although that one takes the cake, in my opinion). There are a number of factors that contribute to un-engaging lessons. Some teachers have monotonous tones, rarely changing the inflection of their voices. Some share powerful truths but speak too softly to hear. Some never make eye contact. Others awkwardly rush through discussion questions. Being an engaging teacher comes naturally to some; others have to work at it over time.

I have found that my teaching style is something that needs constant work, tuning, and refinement. God has given me the great opportunity to engage the hearts of people every week with His eternal truth. I want to make sure that the way I present that truth does not distract from its content. Life-changing, biblical lessons are best taught in a manner that engages everyone in the room—drawing them in, commanding their attention, and stimulating their intellect. Take the next several minutes to browse through the following guidelines for being an engaging small group teacher:

1. *DO NOT* simply read the lesson out of the book. No one in your group comes thinking, "I wish the leader would read the lesson to me today," or, "Wouldn't it be fun if we all took turns reading sections of the lesson guide out loud?" They can read at home. If your teaching consists entirely (or mostly) of you reading word for word from the study guide, I promise you every one in the room is thinking, "I came to be engaged. I can read at home."

The lesson must come to life. It needs to jump off of the page. The only way you can make that happen is to teach it in your own words, while making eye contact with your group members. Get your eyes out of the lesson guide and onto your people.

2. Learn to facilitate group discussion. For some reason, teachers are afraid of dead space. You ask a discussion question. When no one answers in the first five seconds, your first reaction is to fill the dead space. Sometimes you do that by rephrasing the question, sometimes by answering the question for them, and sometimes by just moving on. Don't do this.

When you ask a question, remember that you have already studied the lesson; you already have a desired response in your head. But it often takes a good 10-20 seconds for your group members to process the question, come up with an answer, and begin to put that answer into words that they are confident to share with the group.

DO NOT fill the dead space. Let the question sit with pregnant pause. If they do not understand the question, someone will ask that it be repeated or rephrased. The dead space makes your people as uncomfortable as it makes you; if it is discussion you want in your group, let them be the ones to fill it.

3. Speak loud enough for everyone in the group to hear. Consider the layout of the room. Is the seating arranged in such a way that some are situated far away from you while others are near? Consider the open air in your meeting space: Do you lead a smaller group meeting in a room that is too large, or where the ceilings are very high? You may not have the option of changing meeting rooms, but you do have the option of arranging the set-up where everyone is within an equal distance of your voice. In my experience, circles or semi-circles work best for small group set-up. There, everyone can see each other's face, and all are physically drawn into the lesson by their position in the room.

You need to speak loudly enough that everyone in the room can hear your voice. Maybe that means you need to rearrange some things. Maybe that means you just need to speak a little louder.

4. Change the inflection of your voice as you teach. This comes naturally to some teachers, but takes conscious effort for others. If you tend to speak with a monotone delivery you will need to work at being more dynamic in your speaking.

Every sentence contributes to the developing story of the lesson. When the story is exciting, you need to sound excited. When the story is intense, you need to sound intense. When the story is suspenseful, you need to soften your voice and spread out your words. Allow your delivery to match the tone, emotion, and intensity of the developing lesson.

5. Ask leading questions and facilitate on-topic, guided discussion. People learn when you teach them. But they learn best when they are led into discovering answers for themselves. Your discussion and your questions need to be leading people toward a certain goal or a certain point. If you allow your group members to collaborate together about the lesson then come up with the answers that you hoped they would learn, it will stick with them longer than if you simply lecture and monologue through the main points.

To be honest, this is a teaching skill that takes time to develop. But when you master it, you will begin to see your group members engaged in the lesson like never before. Learn the art of asking leading questions and facilitating on-topic group discussion. This will change the dynamics of your group time by creating a culture of guided group discovery as you engage biblical truth together.

6. Have fun and enjoy your group time. Your group needs to see that you want to be there. Every meeting. Every time. Lesson content can be taught, but commitment to that content and to one another must be caught. This seems so simple, I know. But even if you totally blow it every now and then, if you're enjoyment of the group time is evident it will be contagious.

So smile. Laugh. Enjoy yourself. God didn't redeem you and call you to teach so that you could be a stick in the mud. Don't be irreverent; there are some lessons (and/or portions of lessons) that call for humbled sobriety. But at least, through your facial expression and attitude, make it known that you enjoy and value the group time together.

PRACTICAL TIPS:

• Spend time in preparation on the illustrations and applications, telling them in your own words. Yes, practice them out loud if you need to. Retell the opening illustrations and supporting stories using your own words. Or even better – if you have a personal story or illustration that serves the same purpose as the one in the study guide, tell yours instead. In application, use names of local restaurants, stores, leaders, and parks.

For example, instead of saying, "When you're at the grocery store..." say, "When you're in Kroger..." Instead of saying, "When you're speaking with your pastor..." say, "When you're talking to Pastor Tony..." Instead of saying, "When you are on the softball field..." say, "When you're sitting on the bleachers at Josy

Park..." Make every application as local and personal to your group as possible.

• Facilitating group discussion: After the first person responds, do not shut down the discussion. Usually the first responder's words will trigger a response in another one or two of your group members. Allow your people time to converse back and forth over the question. If you see that someone is trying to get a word in, but for some reason is getting cut off, ask him or her directly, "____ did you have something to add?"

• Learn to affirm responses, even if they are not exactly what you were looking for. Most of the time your brain is working on overdrive as you teach. While the group is answering one discussion question, it is tempting to start thinking about what's coming next. Resist that urge, and instead, be completely in the moment. When someone takes the initiative to speak up and answer a question, they need to be affirmed.

If you will honestly listen, very often your group members will come up with thoughts that add to your lesson—many times in ways you did not even consider. React to those statements.

Say, "Wow, that's good," or "I didn't think of that." Other times, a group member's response to you or to another group member will be straight out of left field. Still... listen and affirm. At a very minimum, say something like, "Thank you for sharing," then either gently redirect the conversation or move on to the next question/teaching point. If you do not affirm responses, people will stop responding.

• Deal with the discussion hog. Sometimes one or two people tend to dominate the discussion time. If this happens every week, it has been my experience that the only way to deal with it is to catch them privately and speak to them about it one on one. Never be condemning. Instead, celebrate the fact that this person wants to share and always has something to add. Then explain that it's your desire to get some of the other group members engaged in discussion. Explain the importance of collaboration in learning. Show how this person can help by allowing others time to answer the questions first.

In the moment, while you are teaching, a helpful tool for opening up discussion to more than one or two people is to affirm and acknowledge them while asking for others to participate. For example: If Suzie has answered

2-3 questions in a row, when you ask the next question say something like, "Anyone other than Suzie want to take a shot at it? – Suzie gets a gold star today (jokingly of course)... I just want to see if anyone else is paying attention."

• Record yourself teaching on a video or audio device. I know, no one likes to watch themselves on camera. You may even be getting sick to your stomach just thinking about it. But I promise, this will be an invaluable adventure in refining your teaching skills. Go back and watch/listen not only for the content, but for the delivery.

Ask yourself: (1) Does the inflection of my voice match the changing tones of the lesson? (2) Do I sound/look like I am reading straight from the study guide? (3) Did I allow my people time to process discussion questions and answer them? (4) Did I affirm answers to discussion questions appropriately? (5) Do I sound/look like I am happy to be there?

• As you study each week, ask yourself questions about the text. This will help you anticipate questions your group members may have. Try to think about the lesson from the perspective of your group members. As you study, write down the questions you think they may ask. Then find answers to those questions so that you can be prepared to deal with them if they arise.

There is no need to say, "I thought you might ask that," or anything of the sort. The point is not to show off your superior intellect, but simply to be prepared for explanation from every angle. Thinking circumspectly in preparation lends itself to creative listening and leading during delivery.

It is a great joy to pour Scripture into the lives of God's people week after week. Be sure that your delivery is more than informational. Work to make it transformational. Don't just speak truths into the ears of attentive learners. Engage their very hearts with the lesson content week after week.

The Scripture verse that opens this chapter, from Romans 15:13, is a prayer that God would fill the reader with joy and peace so that hope might overflow "by the power of the Holy Spirit." Hope is such a powerful thing. Most weeks, it is hope for which your small group members come looking. Their jobs are draining. Their home lives are a wreck. Their relationships are rocky. Hope is what they need.

As a teacher of God's eternal truth, filled with the joy of the Lord, hope should be oozing from your life. Every word of every lesson should be dripping with the hope of God's goodness and grace found in a relationship with Jesus Christ. In fact, your spiritual saliva glands should be moistening right now at the thought. This is a hope that needs to be engaging and appealing to all who enter through your doors. So give it all you've got. Refine your teaching skills. Work at this. Be engaging.

NOTES:

Chapter 5
Be Intentional about Fellowship

*"Every day they devoted themselves to
meeting together in the temple complex,
and broke bread from house to house.
They ate their food with joyful and sincere
hearts, praising God and enjoying the favor
of all the people. Every day the Lord added to
their number those who were being saved."*
Acts 2:46-47

Something amazing happens when God's people gather together. In the words of Dietrich Bonhoeffer, we are to "meet one another as God has met us in Christ." That is, with forgiveness, acceptance, and a peculiar love. When we come to accept the radical nature of our vertical relationship with God, we must also learn to accept the radical nature of our horizontal relationships with one another.

Christlike love is unnatural among men. It is so unnatural that it must be super-natural. Our fellowship in Christ should turn the heads of the watching world. It is by this peculiar love for one another, Jesus said, that the world would know that we are His disciples (John 13:35). Our selfless devotion to one another, on full display in the fellowship of the saints, is something the world can never know apart from Christ. Especially through the first several chapters of Acts, genuine biblical fellowship was on full display in the early church.

The early church was so effective. Notice from the verses which began this chapter that the frequency with which God added to their numbers was directly proportional to the frequency with which they fellowshipped together—every day. Why is that? There's something special about the genuine biblical fellowship of believers in Jesus Christ. If you cross-reference this verse with John 17:21, you might begin to see the gravity with which our biblical fellowship impacts our testimony for Christ.

In a world of hatred, division, back-biting, and cliquishness, the fellowship of the redeemed should stand out. When we get together as Christians it should teach the world some things about unity, togetherness, commonality, friendship, love, and joy. So evidently abnormal should our fellowship be that it sparks a keen interest from those who are not Christians. The way we enjoy each other's company and share our lives together should testify to the watching world that this Jesus/Gospel thing is the real deal.

Here are some ways that your small group can model the fellowship of the church in Acts 3, and begin to show the world around you the uniqueness of togetherness in Christ Jesus.

1. Intentionally schedule times for fellowship with your small group. The key word in this chapter's title is "intentional." As the leader of your group, if you do not intentionally schedule times for group fellowship, it will not happen. My experience has shown that all small groups—whether children, youth, young adults, median adults, or senior adults—need regularly scheduled times of fellowship at least once every month. I generally require small group leaders to schedule fellowships at least once every quarter, but encourage them to do so once every month.

Sometimes these times of fellowships are

well organized and planned, such as Christmas parties or beginning of the year parties. Sometimes they are very loosely organized such as meeting for lunch at a particular restaurant or sending a quick text out to play volleyball at the church. Mark this down... your group members have busy lives; they will NOT stay connected to each other unless you are intentional about providing opportunities for them to do so.

2. Make it your business to connect group members/guests to one another. Some people in your small group will have natural affinities toward some others in your group. They may share a similar occupation, have complimentary personalities, or enjoy the same hobbies. Especially when there is a guest, new member, or disconnected member in your group, be intentional about connecting him or her with one or two others in your group.

As the leader, you usually know what group members are passionate about, the ages of their children or grandchildren, their occupations, or their hobbies. Use your knowledge of your group members' lives to build bridges between them. Ask questions of first time guests toward this end, then introduce/connect them to members of the group who have common affinities. Most small group members stay connected over time because they develop deep, Christ-centered relationships with others in the group. Rejoice in that. Encourage it. Facilitate it.

3. Keep an eye/ear out for signs of discord among group members. You cannot solve their problems—that is true. Nor should you. Part of growing up in Christ is learning how to love and serve one another through conflict. Don't rob your group members of the opportunity for growth by stepping into their conflict too early (see Matthew 18:15-17). Also, don't rob them of the opportunity for growth by neglecting to be a confidential voice of counsel when needed. But you can be attentive to their discord, pray for/with them through it, and be a voice of biblical reason when appropriate.

Guess what: your group members are real people with real problems. They will butt heads. Their personalities will clash. And they will bring their discord into your weekly gatherings and planned fellowships. Satan will do everything he can to sow seeds of discord in your group. But the love of God covers a multitude of sins. When forgiveness and restoration happens within your group setting, it can be a powerful moment. Do your best to facilitate peace through the discord and to promote forgiveness and restoration. Then, when healing comes, rejoice in it.

4. Constantly encourage your group members to fellowship with one another even outside the boundaries of your small group meetings and planned opportunities. The church in Acts did not have well-structured systems for fellowship. They just loved each other deeply and enjoyed each other's company wherever and whenever possible. Members of several small groups at our church sit together in the bleachers at football, volleyball, baseball, and basketball games. We invite others to join us, of course.

The people of our community assume that we enjoy each other's company when we are the church gathered. But it speaks volumes when they see us enjoying each other's company when we are the church scattered.

PRACTICAL TIPS:

• Use social media to celebrate genuine biblical fellowship. Chapter 6 will deal more specifically with social media tools for internal connection, but here, recognize that social media can be a powerful tool for celebrating your group's fellowship so the unchurched in your community can see. When unchurched people in your area begin to see the genuine fellowship that your group enjoys, they will want to be a part of it.

Post public pictures of your group's gatherings. Tag group members. Tag or #hashtag your city, county, or the particular public place of your meeting. Celebrate memorable moments in your weekly studies or monthly gatherings. Encourage your group members to mention your small group lessons or gatherings on their social media accounts. Let your community see that fellowship in this group is real.

• Set a specific day of the month/quarter for group fellowships. If your group plans to fellowship the first Sunday night of every month, or the second Tuesday morning, or every fifth Sunday afternoon, the hardest part is already taken care of (trying to set a date/time). You do not have to do the same thing or go to the same place every time (although that may be beneficial to your group—you decide). But keeping the same recurring day/time can be a tremendous advantage for encouraging regular group fellowship.

• Do something fun. You have a weekly Bible study time already. And you pray for one another in those meetings, and between them. Make your times of planned group fellowship fun and enjoyable. Laugh together. Play together. Cut up together. Don't be boring. If you feel the need to have a devotion or prayer time at one or all of your group fellowships, that's fine. But don't forget to actually fellowship, too. That's the point of these gatherings.

• Seek direction and counsel from your pastor, discipleship pastor, deacon, or church counselor when you become aware of conflict in your group. DO NOT seek advice about members of your small group from other members of your small group, as this will inevitably lead to the spreading of the conflict instead of the concealing of it (see Proverbs 17:9). Your spiritual leaders are there to support you, encourage you, equip you, resource you, and advise you. It is their great privilege to help you through the process of reconciliation within your group when needed.

Fellowship God's way is a powerful thing. It breaks down fortified walls. It builds us together. It binds us together. By our fellowship (our oneness), we testify to the world the truth of the gospel (Jn. 17:21). How sad that discord in the Body of Christ often drives people away from the Person of Christ. Your group needs to be different.

Your group needs to raise the bar for genuine, biblical fellowship. And you need to be the one to lead this change. In Chapter 6 we will turn our attention to staying connected with your group members throughout the week.

NOTES:

Keep Connected with your Group Members

"The report of your obedience has reached everyone. . . . Timothy, my coworker, and Lucius, Jason, and Sosipater, my fellow countrymen, greet you. I Tertius, who wrote this letter, greet you in the Lord. Gaius, who is host to me and to the whole church, greets you. Erastus, the city treasurer, and our brother Quartus greet you."
Romans 16:19-23

In Romans 16:19-23, Paul had his scribe Tertius list eight names that would have likely been familiar to his readers. They had been estranged from one another for quite some time. As Paul writes to the Romans of deep doctrinal concerns and high theology, he is sure to include reference to personal connections that would encourage and strengthen his readers. They needed this. They needed to know that their brothers and sisters in Christ were still engaged in kingdom work. They needed to know that they were not left alone in their own circles. They needed to know that reports of their own faithfulness to Christ had reached the ears and the hearts of their brothers far away. There is encouragement and mutual joy in staying connected.

When your group members leave the meeting area every week, they are immediately thrust back into a world far from God. To make matters worse, usually they are thrust back into this world apart from one another. Together in your weekly group setting they are confident and secure in their faith. But isolated from each other in their workplaces, homes, and social circles, they are often marginalized or ostracized because of their faith in Christ. Sometimes this is true in very small ways. Other times, it is as real and evident as anyone could imagine. The spiritual connection that your group members have with one another must be one that is felt not just in a room together for one hour on the weekends, but throughout the week, every week.

In Paul's day, handwritten letters were the only means of connection while individuals were separated from one another. Today, technology makes this much more convenient. You have at your disposal several tools for connection that, when used appropriately, can keep your group connected in meaningful and powerful ways throughout the week. These tools for connection can strengthen and encourage your group members between meetings. You would be wise to use them and stay connected.

Consider the following current resources for staying connected with your group members throughout the week:

1. Social Media. Some of our church's small groups create a "Page" for their group on Facebook, or a special account or hashtag for their group on Twitter or Instagram. This has proved to be an invaluable way to make announcements, plan events, and request specific and timely prayer. The day before (and the day of) group meetings, a leader will often post a synopsis of the upcoming lesson and get group members and guests thinking about the topic or Scripture at hand.

Use thoughtful discretion when

communicating on social media. It is NEVER the place for correction or disagreement. Live by this rule for your group's social interaction: public praise, private correction. In training, I tell leaders that everything on social media needs to be positive. If it is informational, it needs to be communicated with excitement. If prayerful, with expectation. If Scripture, with love and encouragement. Today, social media can quickly become a place to "vent" or complain. Do not let that happen in direct connection with your small group.

2. Text Messaging. When I was a kid, "text" was a noun. Now it is also a verb. This symbol [#] was a number sign. Now it is also a hashtag. Times change. And with those changes come new ways to stay connected.

One-to-one text messages are a great way to send a quick "praying for you" note to one of your group members. If you know of a job interview, doctor's appointment, or big presentation, send your group member a text letting them know you've prayed for them.

Group texts can also be a valuable asset. They are a very quick and effective way to disseminate information. Last minute changes to a schedule can make use of group texting.

Quick prayer requests can find immediate encouragement in group texting. Text messaging has many potential benefits for your group... However, be sure to give attention to the second bullet point below— under "PRACTICAL TIPS"—regarding two universal rules for text messaging.

3. Email. Techno-savvy individuals born in the 1950's through the early 1980's use email regularly (there are, of course, exceptions in your group). You can send emails to all of your group members and encourage them to "reply all" if they would like the whole group to be included, or they can reply only to you. You will have some group members whose preferred method of communication is email.

However, email is work for me. My email inbox is my to-do list for work. In fact, I literally just emailed myself something that I need to take care of tomorrow when I sit down at my desk. So keep in mind that while email is effective and useful for some, it is not the preferred method of communication for others.

4. Phone Call, Personal Visit. It's always best to call first and ask when might be a good time to visit. Today, people's homes are more like private retreats than open invitations. But it is often very meaningful to simply see the face of someone who honestly cares about you, or to at least just hear their voice.

Respect the private space of your group members. Be sensitive to their boundaries. But consider how a phone call or personal visit might be encouraging to them. For some, personal visits and phone calls are the only way you will make meaningful contact.

5. An Old-Fashioned, Handwritten Letter/Card. Even with all of our technology and all of our fast-paced living, there is still nothing more encouraging than a hand-written note or card received through traditional mail. Every week I sit at my desk and write between 3-5 personal notes to individuals. When I pastored a local congregation, those notes were written to church members or community officials. Now they are usually to pastors across the state, or to coworkers. A handwritten letter or card is a very powerful tool for connecting with people and letting them know that you care.

PRACTICAL TIPS:

• On social media, make calculated use of

hashtags [#] for your group. Place it before (with no spaces) a key word that is unique to your group, and have your group members use it whenever they post things about your church or small group. This generates ongoing acknowledgement that something is happening in your group/church.

When the hashtag is clicked on a social media platform, it will redirect the user (clicker) to a separate page where every post including that hashtag can be seen in one news feed. At a church I pastored in East Texas, we used hashtags such as #ABCLLYOUTH #ABCKids #WeAreOne #ABCPreTeenCamp #ABCLovelady and more.

• When texting, abide by these two rules:

➢ The 9 to 9 Rule. Do not text anyone before 9am or after 9pm. This will keep you in good favor with most of your people, especially those who work out of the home, have children, or like to sleep late. If one of your group members works nights, be sensitive to his or her schedule as well.

➢ The Limited Group Reply Rule. Do not promote or perpetuate ongoing replies to a group message. It is tempting to be funny or witty, or to banter back and forth. But every message anyone sends in an open group message alerts every other person through an audible noise or vibration. What you think is cute and funny can quickly turn annoying or even disrespectful. On your smartphone, you can turn off "Group Replies" in your settings. This way, when someone responds to the group message, it is sent only to you. If the thread needs discussion more than one or two replies deep, consider using email, a phone call, or a face-to-face meeting.

• When someone in your group misses two meetings in a row, be sure to call them. Nothing says "We don't really miss you" like forgetting to follow up with someone who has been MIA for two weeks. Do not guilt them into returning, and be careful not to come across as disappointed. Rather, simply acknowledge that they are missed and you hope to see them again soon. Your people want to know that they are loved, and missed. So love them, miss them, and let them know.

• Every month or two, send out hand-written cards or letters to some of your group members.

Emails, phone calls, text messages, and social media are great, but even in the 21st Century, nothing beats a hand written note. It can be very simple: *"Hey, just wanted to drop you a quick line to let you know that I've been thinking about you and praying for you. I sure am thankful that you're part of our small group. Love ya!"* Include a sentence or two about specific things you've been praying them through: *"Been lifting you up in prayer, trusting the Lord for peace and confidence in your upcoming job interview."*

My handwriting is atrocious, so I usually try to keep my handwritten notes short. I once hand-wrote a letter to a young teenager whose brother had recently taken his own life. The timing of my letter's arrival was crucial, so I actually paid almost $100 to ship this 8.5x11 sheet of paper to him overnight. Months later the young man thanked me with tears in his eyes: "Bro. Tony, your letter meant so much to me. I couldn't read your handwriting so I was going to have someone read it to me when I got home but I think someone threw it away. But still, your letter really meant a lot to me." That was the $100 hand-written letter that was never read. The actual words on the page didn't mean nearly as much as the fact that they were written and sent with love.

• Don't just connect with your people yourself—be sure to facilitate ongoing connection between your group members. Sometimes you have to intentionally go to one of your people to ask them to step over and meet or connect with someone else: *"Hey Bob, Johnny really seems to be disconnected lately. I think he's struggling through some things. Would you please make and effort to connect with him today sometime before you leave, and just offer some encouragement and let him know that you're here for him if he ever needs anything?"* As the small group leader, you don't have to be the one to own all of the interpersonal connections. Just be the bridge builder, who gets people connected to each other.

Your people want so much more than information. They want connection. They don't just need to know that following Jesus is true, they need to see and feel that it is real. The second half of the Greatest Commandment (Mark 12:30-31) is necessarily lived out in the context of Christian community—a perfect display case for the authenticity of biblical fellowship. Timely connections build a solid foundation for spiritual growth within a group of believers. As they walk through life shoulder-to-shoulder, the reality of the truth they claim is on full display.

In most churches, if someone comes to Christ and is baptized but does not join an active small group within the first 6-8 months, he or she will fall away within a year or two. Make an effort to connect with people, to stay connected with them, and to get them connected to others in the group. They are your ministry. Life is too hard to do alone. So do it together, on purpose. Get connected, and stay connected.

NOTES:

CHAPTER 7
Be Missional

"Go, therefore, and make disciples of all nations, baptizing them in the name of the Father and of the Son and of the Holy Spirit, teaching them to observe everything I have commanded you. And remember, I am with you always, to the end of the age."
Matthew 28:19-20

Groups that lack direction and purpose become stagnant, and stagnancy is not conducive to the growth of anything healthy. I grew up tight-line fishing in the Comite River, down in South Louisiana. The prize catch was the blue catfish, a fighter on the end of a fishing line, and a real treat drawn fresh out of the frying pan. When the river overflowed, it flooded several smaller ponds around its banks.

After the flooding subsided, the water level in the river returned to normal and the ponds were isolated again.

In only a matter of weeks, the fish left in those ponds would turn belly-up because stagnant water, without vegetation and cut off from a refreshing flow, cannot maintain healthy oxygen levels over time. Even if you could snag a fish in one of those stagnant ponds, you wouldn't want to eat it because it would be riddled with parasites.

After not catching much off the riverbank one evening, I remember telling my brother we should go fish one of those ponds. He refused and said, "Tony, nothing good grows there."

Your group needs to be a moving stream, constantly headed in the same direction together. There needs to be a purpose—a vision—to unite them and keep them moving forward together. Groups that become stagnate ponds are only inviting spiritual rot and decay. Where there is movement and life, healthy spiritual growth is made possible. But where there is only stagnation and complacency, well, nothing good grows there.

Luckily for you, purpose is not something you have to come up with on your own. It is built in to your role as a spiritual leader within the Body of Christ. All you have to do is constantly call their attention to the flowing river of the Great Commission, and provide practical and meaningful opportunities for them to jump in together.

Being a follower of Jesus is more than simply loving Him, or approving of Him. It's about adopting His mission as our own. And what is the mission of our Lord? At the beginning of Mark's Gospel, the first recorded words of Jesus are these: "The time is fulfilled, and the kingdom of God has come near. Repent and believe in the good news [(the gospel)]!"

After the resurrection Jesus passed on this mission to His disciples. The opening quote for this chapter is what's often referred to as "the Great Commission," from the end of Matthew's Gospel. All three synoptic gospels and The Acts record some form of this statement. In it, Jesus confers authority and responsibility on His followers to engage in His mission to reach the lost with the message of the gospel then disciple them in the faith.

If you thought your small group existed for the sole benefit of its members, think again. Your group is a mission-sending organization. In fact, the small group structure of your church is the best framework the church has for mission and outreach. As your group's leader, you are a manager of this strategy to reach lost and unchurched people in your area. In his book *Sunday School in HD*, Allan Taylor wrote it this way: "Sunday School is the church's strategy to reach lost and unchurched people!"

Every week a number of people gather around you to be filled up, challenged, and encouraged. Then they are sent out to go to the lost in your area with Christ's feet, to serve them with Christ's hands, to love them with Christ's heart, to think of them with Christ's mind, and to speak to them with Christ's voice.

Your small group is the front line for gospel-centered mission in your area. Make sure they own this. And as their leader, learn how to mobilize them for the mission. Here are some things you would be wise to consider in order to be effective in mobilizing your people for Christ's mission.

1. Be evangelistic yourself. It is impossible to lead your group members to do something that you are not doing yourself. Leader, you serve as their model. You are a visible picture of the end product. I promise that if you do not regularly share your faith with lost people, your group members will not, either. In

2 Timothy 4:5, Paul did not ask his young protégé if he had the gift of evangelism. He simply instructed Timothy to "do the work of an evangelist." To the Corinthians, he instructed, "Follow me as I follow Christ," (1 Corinthians 11:1).

Make the commitment to regularly share Christ with lost people, and invite them to your small group. Share your wins and your works-in-progress with the group, then invite group members to share theirs as well.

2. Provide evangelism training opportunities for your group members. There are so many good resources out there to help with this. The Southern Baptists of Texas Convention has the "One Cross APP," free from the APP Store, with which your people can share the gospel with lost souls in over 100 languages, through prerecorded video gospel presentations. The North American Mission Board has a free APP entitled "Life Conversation Guide" (or "3 Circles") that will enable your people to walk through the gospel with someone simply and concisely using their smartphone. Teach your group the Roman Road, or "The Way of the Master." Take them through J. Mack Stiles' short book entitled *Evangelism*, from the *9 Marks* series. William (Billy) Fay has a more extensive process in his *Sharing Jesus Without Fear* approach. Just do *SOMETHING*! Equip them to share the gospel with people outside the walls of your small group gathering, and celebrate their sharing every chance you get.

3. In *every* meeting, occasionally turn the focus off of your group and onto their coworkers, friends, and family members who need Jesus. If all you ever talk about is the people who are in your chairs, you will create and facilitate an inwardly focused culture. But if you are constantly bringing their attention to the lost and unchurched, encouraging and challenging your people to reach them, you will facilitate a culture of outwardly-focused, missionally-minded gospel propagation.

4. As a small group, organize quarterly, mission-minded outreach events in your community and beyond. Bake cookies for the school teachers and deliver them with handwritten cards affirming the teachers and encouraging them with Scripture and prayer. Pull off a block party in a group member's neighborhood. Organize a prayer-walk for your group. Come up with a creative way to serve your community or your school. Take a mission trip to somewhere far away. When you are actively mission-oriented, you will create a culture of outreach and evangelism within your small group.

5. Invest in new leaders within your group, and prepare to multiply your small group by planting a new group in your church. Statistically, the best way for a church's small group structure to grow is to plant new groups. But where do new groups come from? They come from existing groups! Under the supervision of your church's pastor or discipleship leader, when your group grows to 15-20 regular attenders be sure to look for that person or that couple who may be a promising small group leader in the future.

Pray that God would reveal these people to you. Allow them to teach the lesson from time to time. Meet with them privately and discuss the possibility of releasing them to start a new group. When the time comes, talk with 2-3 other families who will join them in this pursuit. Devote a meeting one day to laying hands on these individuals as a small group, commissioning them to this new missional work.

Have your remaining group members pray for them regularly and write encouraging cards to them as they embark on this new journey. Then as your group continues to grow, do it again. And again. And again.

PRACTICAL TIPS:

• Make sure there are empty chairs at every group meeting. This sets up the room to expect guests. Nothing says "you're not welcome here" or "we're full" like someone walking into your small group meeting when there are no spots available for seating. If your group has not seen any guests in a while, call their attention to the open chairs. Pray over those chairs together, asking God to fill them.

• Help one of your group members organize and lead a Bible study in their home, for the families in their neighborhood. Listen to how your group members talk about the families in their neighborhood. If they have been reaching out to them with faith-talk (spiritual conversations), suggest a Bible study in your group member's home. Provide materials. Meet with your group member regularly to discuss the lessons and offer suggestions for leading the group. Have others in your small group prepare snacks for these weekly neighborhood meetings. Celebrate and pray over this work every single week in your small group meeting. And pray, together, for a time when those in the neighborhood Bible study will either be assimilated into your small group or launch a new one of their own.

• When you talk to group members, ask them about the lost and unchurched people God has put in their paths lately. God has given each of your group members a circle of influence that you do not have. They connect with people every day with whom you do not—cannot—connect. Ask them about the spiritual conversations they are having with these people in their circles. Pray together for their salvation.

In doing this, you will make evangelism and outreach more than a large group idea. Instead, it will become a one-to-one reality. Encourage your people to see how their weekly one-to-one missional work fits into the larger picture of the group's (and the church's) evangelism and outreach strategy.

• Occasionally ask open ended questions in your group gathering to the effect of "Why are we here?" "What is our purpose?" or "How does our small group fulfill the Great Commission?" True, biblical discipleship always gives way to dedicated gospel witness. If the climate of your group rests on issues of spiritual growth without challenging its members toward evangelism and outreach, you're doing something wrong. Yes, you, the group leader. You are doing something wrong. Be sure that every group discussion includes some level of missional/evangelistic reflection or challenge. This is your responsibility as its leader—to equip, resource, and mobilize the people under your care to take the gospel message out of the walls of the church and into the lives of those who are far from God.

In Matthew 9:37-38, Jesus challenges His disciples toward the harvest of lost souls: "The harvest is abundant, but the workers are few. Therefore, pray to the Lord of the harvest to send out workers into His harvest." Little did The Twelve know that they would be the workers that Jesus (the Lord of the Harvest – see Rev. 14:14-16) would send out into the fields. In Chapter 10 He gives them authority, and some rules for the road. In Chapter 11, He sends them out.

As a small group leader, you are to be about the business of resourcing, equipping, and releasing your people every single week, to take the message of the gospel to a world that is far from God. This world is in their homes, at their schools, in their workplaces, on their baseball fields, in the basketball bleachers, and in line at the grocery store.

Everywhere your people go, they should be on the lookout for people who might fit into your small group's age range or certain affinity. They should be asking themselves, "How can I engage this person for kingdom purposes?" while praying for God to open doors of conversation that might lead to gospel witness and church invitation.

But you, leader, are the one who sets the tone for evangelism and outreach in your small group. So if you are to be an effective small group leader, you must be missional. And you must lead your people to be missional as well.

NOTES:

Conclusion

I have had the great joy of both sitting under and coaching many excellent small group leaders through the years. I'll admit that some seem to fit the role naturally, as if it comes effortlessly to them. The vast majority of effective small group leaders I have known, however, are those who have developed slowly over time. Don't be discouraged if this seems like a lot of work. No one expects you to be perfect, just progressing. Carve out one or two of the insights in this book that stuck out as you read, and work on them. Give yourself some grace. And some time.

You have, most likely, sat under some excellent small group leaders in your time, too. I challenge you to take just a moment and write down some reflective observations that you admired about him or her.

What was it about his/her teaching that was so captivating?

_____
_____
_____

How did he/she make everyone in the room feel like an invaluable part of the group experience?

_____
_____
_____

How did he/she organize and facilitate group fellowship?

_____
_____
_____

Did the class have a sense of direction and purpose? If so, what factors contributed to that?

_____
_____
_____

Healthy reflection is a powerful tool in a leader's personal development. Learn from both the positive and the negative examples of your past, and from your own experiences as well. Ultimately, however, there is just one example you should emulate as a small group leader.

PRAY. The Lord Jesus was a great prayer warrior. He taught his disciples how to pray (Luke 11:1-13), and he modeled faithful, fervent prayer in front of them (John 17). He regularly withdrew from the crowds to spend time alone with the Father in prayer (Mark 1:35, Luke 22:39). He thanked His Father for hearing His requests, even before they were answered (John 11:41). He prayed intercessory prayers, aimed at the struggles of specific individuals (Luke 22:32). Jesus prayed for his small group. Pray like Jesus.

TEACH. From an early age, the Lord Jesus treasured the Word of God in His heart. As a young boy, Mary and Joseph found him in the temple, where those who heard his questions and answers were astounded by his biblical insight (Luke 2:47). He frustrated the temptations of Satan by skillfully wielding the Word of God (Matthew 4:1-11). He taught with such understanding and authority that the spiritual leaders took note and even the unclean spirits obeyed Him (Mark 1:27). He corrected (Matthew 15:7-9). He clarified (Matthew 22:43-46). He rebuked (Mark 11:17). He affirmed (Luke 7:27). Jesus taught the content of God's Word clearly and compellingly. Teach like Jesus.

MANAGE TIME. Our Lord had a clear understanding of the urgency of his time (Mark 1:15). He called his small group's attention to time's limitation (Matthew 25:13), and the necessity of making the most of it (John 9:4). Christ came at the appointed time (Galatians 4:4). He was a man of discipline and order (Luke 22:39), but always saw people as the ministry, not the problem (Matthew 9:20-22). Jesus was very aware of time's allowances and limitations, and he knew the value of every single moment. Manage time like Jesus.

ENGAGE. Jesus was also a masterful communicator. He spoke to the heart, not just the head (Mark 10:17-22). He asked leading questions and guided his small group into the truth (Matthew 16:13-18). In his teaching, Jesus used object lessons (John 4:1-14), hyperbole (Mark 9:47), shock-and-awe (John 6:53), analogy (Matthew 16:11), and parables (Matthew 13:1-

50). Needless to say, Jesus's teaching style was engaging, diverse, and relevant. Jesus was engaging deliverer. Engage like Jesus.

FELLOWSHIP. Knowing full well the weight of His ministry and His message, the Lord Jesus had an inviting personality, and enjoyed sincere fellowship within his small group. People wanted to be around Jesus so badly, they would do just about anything to get to where he was going (Mark 6:32-33). He reclined at the table with Matthew and his unpopular tax collector friends (Matthew 9:10). He cooked a fisherman's breakfast for his small group and fellowshipped with them on the shore (John 21:9-14). As His small group met one evening, He turned an awkward, ominous moment into an elaborate display of the importance of loving one another (John 13:28-35). Jesus knew how to have healthy fellowship with people. Fellowship like Jesus.

CONNECT. Jesus didn't just teach life lessons and provide moral coaching. He did life with his disciples. He walked with them (John 12:35), cried with them (John 11:35), celebrated with them (Mark 6:30), and sang with them (Matthew 26:30). When He was absent from them, He longed to be with them (John 14:1-4, Matthew 26:29). Jesus's ministry to His small group was more than collaboration. It was connection. Connect like Jesus.

BE MISSIONAL. From His first moment to His last, the Lord's earthly leadership was directional. He called His disciples to follow Him with a clearly stated purpose (Matthew 4:19). Everything He did in life and ministry, He did while he was on His way somewhere else. And when He spoke His last word to His small group, it was a restatement of the same directional mission to which He originally called them: "Go, make disciples," (Matthew 28:19-20). Jesus's mission was the same mission God has been on since the Fall of Man: to redeem people from every tribe, nation, and tongue (Revelation 5:9). Jesus invited His disciples to jump into the moving stream of His divine purpose. At all times, He led with the mission in mind. Be missional like Jesus.

It is my sincerest prayer that this book has given you a brief theological framework and some practical tools to sharpen your skills as you follow God's call to lead a small group in your church. This is no small task. Your work is vital to the overall health of your local church, and to the kingdom of God as a whole.

So pray like your life depends on it. Teach the content. Manage every moment prudently. Be engaging in your delivery. Commit yourself to genuine biblical fellowship. Connect your people with one another. And keep them all moving forward in the mission.

Give your attention to these seven things. You can. You should. You must, if you are to be effective as a small group leader.

Recommended Resources for Further Study

Berg, Jim. *Changed Into His Image: God's Plan for Transforming Your Life*. Greenville, SC: JourneyForth, 1999.

Fay, William and Linda Shepherd. *Share Jesus Without Fear*. Nashville, TN: B&H Publishing, 1999.

Geiger, Eric, Michael Kelley, and Philip Nation. *Transformational Discipleship: How People Really Grow*. Nashville, TN: B&H Publishing, 2012.

Grenz, Stanley J. *Created For Community: Connecting Christian Belief with Christian Living*. Grand Rapids, MI: Baker Books, 1998.

Parr, Steve R. *Sunday School that Really Works: A Strategy for Connecting Congregations and Communities*. Grand Rapids, MI: Kregal, 2010.

Parr, Steve R. and Tom Crites. *Why They Stay: Helping Parents and Church Leaders Make Investments That Keep Children and Teens Connected to the Church for a Lifetime*. Bloomington, IN: Westbow Press, 2015.

Putnam, Jim. *Real-Life Discipleship: Building Churches that Make Disciples*. Colorado Springs, CO: NavPress, 2010.

Stiles, J. Mack. *Evangelism*. Wheaton, IL: Crossway, 2014.

Taylor, Allan. *Sunday School in HD*. Nashville, TN: B&H Publishing, 2009.

Wolfe, Anthony. *Mile Markers: Stages of Growth Along the Journey Toward Spiritual Maturity*. Castle Rock, CO: Crosslink Publishing, 2016.

Look for these other titles by Dr. Tony Wolfe

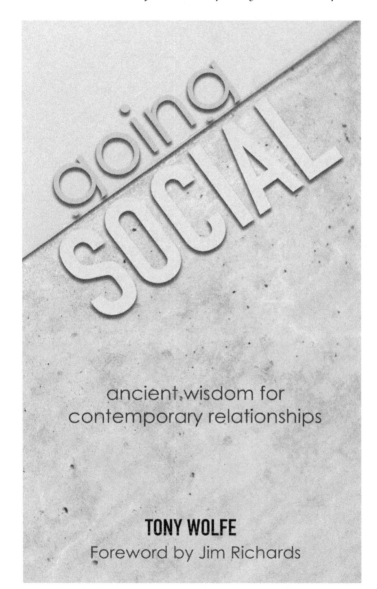

ancient wisdom for
contemporary relationships

TONY WOLFE
Foreword by Jim Richards

Mile Markers

stages of growth along the journey toward spiritual maturity

Dr. Tony Wolfe

www.tonywolfe.net